W9-BLH-918

The Aquinas Lecture, 1990

FIRST PRINCIPLES, FINAL ENDS AND CONTEMPORARY PHILOSOPHICAL ISSUES

Under the auspices of the
Wisconsin-Alpha Chapter of Phi Sigma Tau

by

ALASDAIR MACINTYRE

Marquette University Press
Milwaukee
1990

Library of Congress Catalogue Number: 89-64321.

Copyright 1990

Marquette University Press

ISBN 0-87462-157-7.

Prefatory

The Wisconsin-Alpha Chapter of Phi Sigma Tau, the National Honor Society for Philosophy at Marquette University, each year invites a scholar to deliver a lecture in honor of St. Thomas Aquinas.

The 1990 Aquinas Lecture, *First Principles, Final Ends and Contemporary Philosophical Issues*, was delivered in the Todd Wehr Chemistry Building on Sunday, February 25, 1990 by Alasdair MacIntyre, the McMahon-Hank Professor of Philosophy at the University of Notre Dame.

Professor MacIntyre was born in 1929 and was educated at Queen Mary College of the University of London and at Manchester University. He has taught at various British and American Universities, including Oxford University from 1963 to 1966, the University of Essex from 1966 to 1970, Brandeis University from 1970 to 1972, Boston University from 1972 to 1980, and Wellesley College from 1980 to 1982. Most recently he has taught at Vanderbilt University from 1982 to 1988 and in 1988-1989 at Yale University where he was Henry R. Luce, Jr. Visiting Scholar at the Whitney Humanities Center. Since September of 1988 he has been the McMahon-Hank Professor of Philosophy at the University of Notre Dame.

In 1983 Professor MacIntyre received an honorary Doctorate of Humane Letters from Swarthmore College, and in 1988 he received an honorary Doctorate of Literature from the Queen's University of Belfast. He is a Fellow of the American Academy of Arts and Sciences and served as the President of the Eastern Division of the American Philosophical Association in 1984.

Among his books are: *Marxism: An Interpretation* (1953), *The Unconscious: A Conceptual Analysis* (1958), *Difficulties in Christian Belief* (1959), *A Short History of Ethics* (1966), *Secularization and Moral Change* (1967), *Marxism and Christianity* (1968), *Against the Self-Images of the Age: Essays on Ideology and Philosophy* (1971; repr. 1978), *After Virtue* (1981), and *Whose Justice? Which Rationality?* (1988). He has over one hundred articles and reviews in learned journals, encyclopedias and books.

In 1988 Professor MacIntyre gave the Gifford Lectures at the University of Edinburgh; in 1985 he gave the Richard Peters Lecture at the University of London. Among other special lectures, he has in the past decade delivered the Lindley Lecture at the University of Kansas (1984), the Adams Lecture at Bowdoin College (1983), the Carlyle Lectures at Oxford University (1982) and the Gauss Seminars at Princeton University (1981).

To Professor MacIntyre's distinguished list of publications, Phi Sigma Tau is pleased to add: *First Principles, Final Ends and Contemporary Philosophical Issues*.

FIRST PRINCIPLES, FINAL ENDS AND CONTEMPORARY PHILOSOPHICAL ISSUES

I

Nothing is more generally unacceptable in recent philosophy than any conception of a first principle. Standpoints mutually at odds with each other in so many other ways, of analytic or continental or pragmatic provenance, agree in this rejection. And yet the concept of a first principle seems to have been for Aquinas, just as it had been for Aristotle, and before him for Plato, in itself unproblematic. For both Aquinas and Aristotle, of course, difficult questions do arise about such issues as the relationship of subordinate principles to first principles, the nature of our knowledge of first principles and the differences between the first principles of the different sciences. But in their writings debate even about such complex issues seems always to presuppose as not to be put in question, as never yet having been seriously put in question, the very idea of a first principle.

It is then unsurprisingly in the context of philosophical preoccupations and through the medium of philosophical idioms quite alien to those of either Aristotle or Aquinas that the very idea of a first principle has now been radically put in question, preoccupations which it is, therefore, difficult to address directly from a Thomistic standpoint with only the resources afforded by Aquinas and his predecessors. Hence, it seems that, if this central Aristotelian and Thomistic concept is to be effectively defended, in key part it will have to be by drawing upon philosophical resources which are themselves -- at least at first sight -- as alien to, or almost as alien to, Thomism as are the theses and arguments which have been deployed against it. We inhabit a time in the history of philosophy in which Thomism can only develop adequate responses to the rejections of its central positions in what must seem initially at least to be unThomistic ways.

To acknowledge this is not to suggest that Aquinas's central positions ought to be substantially reworked or revised in some accommodation to the standpoints of those rejections. It is rather that, in order to restate and to defend those positions in something like their original integrity, it is necessary in our time to approach them indirectly through an internal critique of those theses and arguments which have displaced them, a critique dictated by Thomistic ends, but to be carried through in part at least by somewhat unThomistic means.

Yet if such a critique is genuinely to be directed by Thomistic ends it is worth reminding ourselves at the outset just how foreign to contemporary modes and fashions of thought the Aristotelian and Thomistic concept of a first principle is in at least two ways, one concerned with the firstness of first principles, the other with the difference between standard modern uses of the word *'principle'* in English -- and its cognates in other contemporary languages -- and the meaning given to *'principium'* by Aquinas and to *'archê'* by Aristotle. Let me begin with the latter.

'Principium' as a translation of *'archê'* preserves what from a contemporary English-speaking point of view seems like a double meaning. For us a principle is something expressed in language, something which in the form of either a statement or an injunction can function as a premise in arguments. And so it is sometimes for Aquinas who uses *'principium'* of an axiom furnishing a syllogism with a premise (*Commentary on the Posterior Analytics* I, 5) and speaks of a principle as composed of subject and predicate (S.T. I, 17, 3). But Aquinas also uses *'principium'* in speaking of that to which such principles refer, referring to the elements into which composite bodies can be resolved and by reference to which they can be explained as the *'principia'*

of those bodies (*Exposition of Boethius De Trinitate*
V, 4). In fact, *'principium,'* as used by Aquinas,
names simultaneously the principle (in our sense)
and that of which the principle speaks, but not in a
way that gives to *'principium'* two distinct and dis-
crete meanings, although it can be used with either
or both of two distinct references. For when we do
indeed have a *principium*, we have to comprehend
the principle *and* that of which it speaks in a single
act of comprehension; we can only comprehend the
principle *as* it refers us to that of which it speaks and
we can only comprehend that of which it speaks *as*
articulated and formulated in the principle.

   The habits of speech required of us to say
this go against the contemporary linguistic grain. And
certainly sometimes it does no harm to speak of
'principium' as though our contemporary conception
of principle were all that is involved, but we always
have to remember that *'principium,'* like *'archê,'* is a
concept which unites what contemporary idiom
divides. A concept with a similar structure is that of
aitia or *causa*. *We* in the idioms of our contemporary
speech distinguish sharply causes from explanations,
but cause is always explanation-affording and *aitia
qua* explanation is always cause-specifying. In both
cases, that of *aitia/causa* and that of
archê/principium the modern question: 'Are you
speaking of what is or of the mind's apprehension
though language of what is?' misses and obscures the

conceptual point, which is that the application of this type of concept, when sufficiently justified, gives expression to a coincidence of the mind with what is, to a certain kind of achievement in the mind's movement towards its goal. So it is that *causa* and *principium* are to be adequately elucidated only within a scheme of thought in which the mind moves towards its own proper end, its *telos*, an achieved state in which it is informed by an understanding of its own progress towards that end, an understanding completed by an apprehension of first principles. The meaning of these expressions is not independent of the context of theory within which they are employed.

In recognizing this we encounter a familiar truth about radical philosophical disagreements. Theory and idiom are to some significant degree inseparable. Insofar as I try to deny your theory, but continue to use your idiom, it may be that I shall be trapped into presupposing just what I aspire to deny. And correspondingly the more radical the disagreement over theory, the larger the possibility that each party will find itself misrepresented in the idioms of its rivals, idioms which exclude rather than merely lack the conceptual resources necessary for the statement of its position. So it has been to some significant degree with Thomism in its encounter with post-Cartesian philosophies.

This linguistic difficulty is reinforced by the barrier posed by the conviction which I noticed at the outset, one shared both by different, often mutually antagonistic schools of contemporary philosophy and by the culture of modernity at large, that no principle is or can be first as such. To treat a principle as a first principle is always, on this view, to choose to do so for some particular purpose within some particular context. So we in one type of formal system may wish to treat as a derived theorem what in another is treated as an axiom. Justificatory chains of reasoning generally terminate with what members of some particular social group are willing, for the moment at least, to take for granted; this type of agreement is all that is necessary to serve our contemporary justificatory purposes. But it is not just that the firstness of first principles has been relativized to social contexts and individual purposes. It is also that the range of such purposes is taken to be indefinitely various. And what the purposes of each of us are to be is taken to be a matter of our individual temperaments, interests, desires and decisions.

This contemporary universe of discourse thus has no place within it for any conception of fixed ends, of ends to be discovered rather than decided upon or invented, and that is to say that it has no place for the type of *telos* or *finis* which provides the activity of a particular kind of being with a goal to which it must order its purposes or fail to achieve its own specific perfection in its activity. And this exclusion of the concept of *telos/finis*, I shall want to suggest, is closely related to the exclusion of the concept of *archê/principium*. Genuinely first principles, so I shall argue, can have a place only within a universe characterized in terms of certain determinate, fixed and unalterable ends, ends which provide a standard by reference to which our individual purposes, desires, interests and decisions can be evaluated as well or badly directed. For in practical life it is the *telos* which provides the *archê*, the first principle of practical reasoning: "Deductive arguments concerning what is to be done have an *archê*. Since such and such is the *telos* and the best. . ." (N.E. VI 1144a32-35), says Aristotle; and Aquinas comments that this reference to the end in the first principle of practical syllogisms has a parallel in the way in which the first principle of theoretical syllogisms are formulated (*Commentary on the Ethics* VI, lect. 10, 17). And it could scarcely be otherwise since the *archai/principia* of theory furnish the theoretical intellect with its specific *telos/finis*. *Archê/principium* and *telos/finis*, so it must seem, stand or fall together.

II

Within distinctively modern schemes of thought they are, of course, taken to have fallen quite some time ago. And when Thomists, therefore, find their central theses concerning *archê/principium* and *telos/finis* rejected within contemporary culture at large as well as within philosophy, it may be tempting to proceed by way of an immediate rejection of the rejection, but this temptation must be resisted. For it will turn out that the considerations which in the context of contemporary discourse are taken to either support or presuppose denials of the possibility of there being either first principles or final ends are in fact theses which for the most part a Thomist should have no interest in denying. What he or she must have the strongest interest in denying are the implications which are commonly nowadays supposed to follow from these.

The first of such theses denies that there are or can be what I shall call epistemological first principles, the type of first principle of which the Cartesian cogito, as usually understood, provides a paradigmatic instance. Such a first principle was required to fulfill two functions. On the one hand, it had to warrant an immediate justified certitude on the part of any rational person who uttered it in the appropriate way, perhaps in the appropriate circumstances. It belongs, that is, to the same class of statements as "I am in pain," "This is red here now" and

"I am now thinking." But, on the other hand, it had, either by itself or as a member of a set of such statements, to provide an ultimate warrant for all our claims to knowledge. Only in virtue of their derivation from it could other statements meet the challenge: How do you know *that*? And the importance of being able to answer this question is not just to rebut those who express scepticism. For since on this view knowledge involves justified certainty and justified certainty requires that, if I genuinely know, I also know that I know, then as a rational person I must be able to answer the question 'How do I know?' in respect of each knowledge claim that I make.

Yet, as by now has often enough been pointed out, no statement or set of statements is capable of fulfilling both these functions. The kind of substantive content required for statements which could function as the initial premises in a deductive justification of the sciences, theoretical or practical, precludes the kind of justified immediate certitude required for this kind of epistemological starting-point, and vice versa. Epistemological first principles, thus conceived, are mythological beasts.

Two kinds of reflection may be provoked in a Thomist by these by now commonplace antifoundational arguments. A first concerns the way in which they leave the Aristotelian or Thomistic conception of *archê/principium* unscathed. For where the protagonists of the type of foundationalist epistemological first principle, which is now for the most part, even if not universally rejected, characterized those principles so that they had to meet two sets of requirements, each of which could in fact only be met by some principle which failed in respect to the other, Aquinas, as a result of having reflected upon both Aristotle and Boethius, distinguished two different types of evidentness belonging to two different kinds of principle (See, for example, S.T. Ia-IIae 94, 2).

There are, on the one hand, those evident principles, the meaning of whose terms is immediately to be comprehended by every competent language-user, such as 'Every whole is greater than its part,' principles which are, therefore, undeniable by any such language-user. There are, on the other hand, principles which are to be understood as evident only in the context of the conceptual framework of some more or less large-scale theory, principles expressed in judgments known as evident only to those with an intellectual grasp of the theoretical framework in which they are embedded, that is, as Aquinas puts it, to the wise. It is such judgments which are used to state first principles with substantive content, and their function and the requirements which they have to meet are very different from those of the former type of principle. We should, of course, note that even the former type of principle can, in the light of its applications, be understood in greater depth by those who are theoretically sophisticated than it is by the merely competent language-user. But with the distinction between what is immediately apprehended, but not substantive in content, and what is substantive in content, but known as evident only through theoretical achievement, the Thomist distinguishes what the protagonist of epistemological first principles misleadingly assimilates and so remains untouched by this thrust at least of contemporary antifoundationalism.

Yet there is an even more fundamental way in which contemporary hostility to epistemological foundationalism misses the point so far as Thomistic first principles are concerned. For if the Thomist is faithful to the intentions of Aristotle and Aquinas, he or she will not be engaged, except perhaps incidentally, in an epistemological enterprise. The refutation of skepticism will appear to him or her as misguided an enterprise as it does to the Wittgensteinian. Generations of neoThomists from Kleutgen onwards have, of course, taught us to think otherwise, and textbooks on epistemology have been notable among the standard impedimenta of neoThomism. What in part misled their writers was the obvious fact that Aquinas, like Aristotle, furnishes an account of knowledge. What they failed to discern adequately was the difference between the

Aristotelian or Thomistic enterprise and the epistemological enterprise.[1]

The epistemological enterprise is by its nature a first-person project. How can *I*, so the epistemologist enquires, be assured that *my* beliefs, *my* perceptions, *my* judgments connect with reality external to them, so that *I* can have justified certitude regarding their truth and error? A radical sceptic is an epistemologist with entirely negative findings. He or she, like other epistemologists, takes him or herself to speak from within his or her mind of its relationship to what is external to it and perhaps alien to it. But the Thomist, if he or she follows Aristotle and Aquinas, constructs an account both of approaches to and of the achievement of knowledge from a third-person point of view. My mind or rather my soul is only one among many and its own knowledge of my self *qua* soul has to be integrated into a general account of souls and their teleology. Insofar as a given soul moves successfully towards its successive intellectual goals in a teleologically ordered way, it moves towards completing itself by becoming formally identical with the objects of its knowledge, so that it is adequate to those objects, objects that are then no longer external to it, but rather complete it. So the mind in finding application for its concepts refers them beyond itself and themselves to what they conceptualize. Hence the double reference of concepts which we already noticed in the cases of *archê/principium* and *aitia/causa*. The mind, actualized in knowledge, responds to the object as the object is and as it would be, independently of the mind's knowledge of it. The mind knows itself only in the second-order knowledge of its own operations and is known also by others in those operations. But even such knowledge when achieved need not entail certitude of a Cartesian sort.

"It is difficult to discern whether one knows or not," said Aristotle (*Posterior Analytics* I, 9, 76a26). And Aquinas glosses this by saying that "It is difficult to discern whether we know from appropriate principles, which alone is genuinely scientific knowing, or do not know from appropriate principles" (*Commentary on the Posterior Analytics*, lib. 1, lect. 18). The contrast with Cartesianism could not be sharper. If, on the view of Aristotle and Aquinas, one genuinely knows at all, then one knows as one would know if one knew in the light of the relevant set of first principles, but one may, nonetheless, genuinely know, without as yet possessing that further knowledge of first principles and of their relationship to this particular piece of knowledge which would finally vindicate one's claim. All knowledge even in the initial stages of enquiry is a partial achievement and completion of the mind, but it nonetheless points beyond itself to a more final achievement in ways that we may not as yet have grasped. Hence, we can know without as yet knowing

that we know, while for the Cartesian, as I remarked
earlier, if we know, we must know that we know,
since for the Cartesian it is always reference back-
wards to our starting-point that guarantees our
knowledge and, hence, it is only through knowing
that we know that we know. By contrast, for the
Thomist our present knowledge involves reference
forward to that knowledge of the *archê/principium*
which will, if we achieve it, give us subsequent knowledge of the knowledge that we now have.

In this relationship of what we now know to
what we do not as yet know, a relationship in which
what we only as yet know potentially is presupposed
by what we already know actually, there is to be
observed a certain kind of circularity. This is not, of
course, the type of circularity the presence of which
vitiates a demonstrative argument. It is the circularity
of which Aquinas speaks in endorsing Aristotle's
view "that before an induction or syllogism is formed
to beget knowledge of a conclusion, that conclusion
is somehow known and somehow not known" (*Commentary on the Posterior Analytics*, lib. 1, lect. 3). The
conclusion which is to be the end of our deductively
or inductively (Aristotelian *epagôgê*, not Humean
induction) reasoned enquiry is somehow already
assumed in our starting-point. Were it not so, that
particular type of starting-point would not be point-
ing us towards this particular type of conclusion
(*Quaestiones Disputatae De Veritate* 11, 1).

Consider an example from the life of practice. Aquinas follows Aristotle in holding that one reason why the young are incapable of adequate reflective moral theorizing is that they have not as yet that experience of actions which would enable them to frame adequate moral and political arguments (N.E. I, 3, 1095a2-3, *Commentary on the Ethics*, lect. 3). But not any experience of human actions will provide adequate premises for sound practical reasoning. Only a life whose actions have been directed by and whose passions have been disciplined and transformed by the practice of the moral and intellectual virtues and the social relationships involved in and defined by such practice will provide the kind of experience from which and about which reliable practical inferences and sound theoretical arguments about practice can be derived. But from the outset the practice of those virtues in an adequately and increasingly determinate way already presupposes just those truths about the good and the best for human beings, about the *telos* for human beings, which it is the object of moral and political enquiry to discover. So the only type of moral and political enquiry through which and in which success can be achieved is one in which the end is to some significant degree presupposed in the beginning, in which initial actualities presuppose and give evidence of potentiality for future development.

This ineliminable circularity is not a sign of
some flaw in Aristotelian or Thomistic conceptions
of enquiry. It is, I suspect, a feature of any large-scale
philosophical system which embodies a conception of
enquiry, albeit an often unacknowledged feature.
And it could only be thought a flaw from a standpoint still haunted by a desire to find some point of
origin for enquiry which is entirely innocent of that
which can only emerge later from that enquiry. It is
this desire -- for an origin which is not an origin --
which plainly haunts much of the work of Jacques
Derrida[2] and which thus informs, even if somewhat
paradoxically, the second major contemporary
philosophical rejection of any substantive conception
of first principles, one very different from its analytic
antifoundationalist counterpart.

The most obvious difference is, of course,
that, whereas the analytic rejection focusses upon
epistemological considerations, the deconstructionist
rejection formulated by Derrida focusses upon
questions of meaning. What set the stage for
Derrida's critique of what he took to be a metaphysical and, therefore, obfuscating understanding of
meaning was the structuralist thesis, developed out of
a particular way of interpreting Saussure, that in the
structures of linguistic systems it is relationships of a
certain kind which determine the identity and meaning of terms and not *vice versa*. It is in and through

binary relationships of opposition and difference that such identity and meaning are constituted.

The stability of meaning is thus taken to depend upon the character of the oppositions and differences between terms. And a key part of Derrida's deconstructive work was to show that the oppositions between pairs of terms crucial to metaphysics, such counterpart pairs as form/matter, sensible/intelligible, and passive/active, seem to collapse into each other insofar as the meaning and application of each term already presupposes the meaning and applicability of its counterpart, and hence no term provides an independent stable, unchanging point of definition for its counterpart. Insofar as this is so, any stable meaning is dependent upon something not yet said, and since these metaphysical oppositions are in the relevant respects no different from the binary oppositions which on this type of poststructuralist view constitute language-in-use in general, it is a general truth that the meaning of what is uttered is always in a similar way dependent on some further not yet provided ground for meaning, but there is no such ground waiting to be attained, so that stable meaning is never achieved. So a deconstructive denial of first principles emerges from an analysis of meaning, as part of the denial of the possibility of metaphysical grounding for *anything*. But why does Derrida believe that there can be no such ground?

It is here that Derrida is open to more than
one reading. For sometimes it seems that it is from
the way in which the terms of his metaphysical pairs
each presuppose the other, so that neither member
of such pairs can provide an independent grounding
for the meaning, identity and applicability of the
other, that Derrida is arguing to the conclusion that
there can be no grounding for metaphysical thought
and theory of the kind which he takes it to require.
But at other times he seems to move from the denial
of the possibility of such a grounding, on occasion
referring us to Heidegger and to Nietzsche, towards
conclusions about the consequent instability of meaning exemplified in such terms.

Yet in either case what Derrida presents us
with is a strange mirror-image inversion of Thomism.
For the Thomist has no problem either with the
notion that, where such pairs as form and matter or
potentiality and act are concerned, each term is and
must be partially definable by reference to the other,
or with the view that when such terms are applied at
some early or intermediate stage in an enquiry the
full meaning of what has been said is yet to emerge
and will only emerge when the relevant set of first
principles is as fully specified as that particular
enquiry requires. Terms are applied analogically, in
respect both of meaning and of use, and the grounding of meaning and use through analogy is by reference to some ultimate *archê/principium*. So that

stability of meaning, on a Thomist view, is tied to a metaphysically conceived ground, just as Derrida asserts, and the denial of that ground, it follows equally for the Thomist and the deconstructionist, could not but issue in systematic instability of meaning. Yet, if the entailments are the same, the direction of the arguments which they inform is, of course, different. So why move in the deconstructive rather than in the Thomistic direction?

To state Derrida's answer to this justly and adequately would require me to go further into the detail of his position than is possible on this occasion. What is possible is to sketch one central relevant deconstructive thesis which may illuminate what is at stake in the disagreement. For Derrida as for deconstructive thought generally, any metaphysically conceived ground, such as an *archê/principium* would supply, would have to function in two incompatible ways. It would have to exist outside of and independently of discourse, since upon it discourse is to be grounded, and it would have to be present in discourse, since it is only as linguistically conceived and presented that it could be referred to. But these are plainly incompatible requirements, the first of which in any case violates Derrida's dictum that there is nothing outside text. (Notice the instructive resemblances between Derrida's denials and Hilary Putnam's attacks on what he calls external or metaphysical realism[3]). So the binary oppositions of meaning cannot be referred beyond themselves to some first principle and meaning must be unstable.

This deconstructive rejection of first principles raises some of the same questions which arise from the analytic antifoundationalist's rejection. To what kind of reasoning is each appealing in justifying and commending their rejection? Is it a kind of reasoning which is itself consistent with those rejections? Or do those rejections themselves destroy any basis for the reasoning which led to them? Consider the impasse into which thought is led by the difficulties involved in two rival types of answers to those questions. On the one hand, it is easy to construe both the analytic antifoundationalist and the deconstructive critic as offering what are taken to be compelling arguments as to the impossibility of grounding either justificatory argument or discourse itself by means of appeal to some set of first principles. But if these arguments have succeeded in respect of cogency, it can surely be only in virtue of their deriving their conclusions from premises which are in some way or other undeniable. Yet the impossibility of such undeniable premises seems to follow from the conclusions of these same arguments. So can those arguments be construed in a way which will avoid self-deconstruction? This is a more than rhetorical question.

On the other hand, if we begin by taking seriously the thought that there are no in principle undeniable premises -- whatever the type of principle -- for substantive arguments, then the undeniability claimed must be of some other kind. But the most plausible attempts hitherto to elucidate the notion of an undeniability for the premises of deconstructive and antifoundationalist argument, which is not an undeniability in principle, have resulted in some conception of an undeniability rooted in some particular kind of social agreement. Characterizations of the nature of the social agreement involved have differed widely: more than one of the rival views contending in this area appeals to Wittgenstein, others to Kuhn, others again to Foucault.

Disagreement on these issues by a multiplicity of contending parties, grounded in their shared rejection of metaphysical first principles, indeed of first principles as such, is pervasive in its effects and manifestations both within academic philosophy and outside it, both in the literary and social scientific disciplines and in the rhetorical modes of the culture at large. In the latter it appears in the now, it seems, perpetually renewed debates over continually reformulated end-of-ideology theses; the end of ideology is in politics what the refutation of metaphysics is in philosophy. Within academia it appears in the unsettled and, as I shall claim, unsettlable debates which are now carried on between historicists and antihistoricists, realists and antirealists, pragmaticists and antipragmaticists.

It is at this point that the Thomist has to resist the temptation of premature self-congratulation. For, if it is indeed the case, as I have suggested, that the Aristotelian and Thomistic conception of *archê/principium* survives unscathed both the analytic antifoundationalist and the deconstructive critique of first principles, it would be all too easy too announce victory. Yet this would be a serious mistake. For it is not so much that Thomism has emerged unscathed from two serious philosophical encounters as that no serious philosophical encounter has as yet taken place. The Thomistic conception of a first principle is untouched by contemporary radical critiques in key part because the cultural, linguistic and philosophical distance between it and them is now so great, that they are no longer able seriously to envisage the possibility of such a conception. If then serious encounter is to occur, and the Thomistic understanding of the tasks of natural human reason functioning philosophically makes such encounter mandatory, it can only occur insofar as Thomism can speak relevantly of and to those critiques and the debates which arise out of them, even if they cannot speak of it. The question which I am posing, then, is that of what light the Aristotelian and Thomistic conception of *archê/principium* can throw on such critiques and debates. But a necessary pre-

liminary to that question is a more adequate statement of what that conception is and involves.

III

Aquinas introduced his commentary on the
Posterior Analytics by distinouishing the task of
analyzing judgments within a science, with a view to
explaining their warrant and the kind of certitude to
which we are entitled by that warrant, from the task
of giving an account of investigation. In so dis-
tinguishing he pointed towards the resolution of a
problem about what Aristotle was trying to achieve
in the *Posterior Analytics* which has engaged the
attention of some modern commentators.

This problem arises from an evident contrast between the account of the structure of scientific understanding and of how it is achieved which is
provided in the *Posterior Analytics* and the way in
which Aristotle carries out his own scientific
enquiries in the *Physics* and in the biological
treatises. If, as has often enough been assumed by
modern commentators, the *Posterior Analytics* is
Aristotle's theory of scientific method, while the
Physics and the biological treatises are applications
of Aristotle's scientific method, then the discrepancy
between the former and the latter is obvious and
striking. What the first expounds is just not what the
second practices. There have indeed been scholars
who have, nonetheless, attempted to deny that there

is any problem here. But their arguments have not
withstood the test of debate, and it would now be
generally agreed that, whatever the method or
methods of enquiry put to work in the *Physics* and
the biological treatises, they are not the methods
described in the *Posterior Analytics*. How then is the
discrepancy to be explained?

Is it perhaps that Aristotle changed his mind
some time after writing the *Posterior Analytics*? Is it,
as some scholars have maintained, that the *Posterior
Analytics* is an account only of the mathematical sciences? Or is it, as Jonathan Barnes has argued,[4] after
decisively refuting this latter suggestion, that the
Posterior Analytics is not designed to teach us how to
acquire knowledge, but rather how to present knowledge already achieved, that is, that the *Posterior
Analytics* is a manual for teachers? There is no problem in agreeing with much of what Barnes says in
favor of this view, provided that we do not take the
criteria of sound scientific demonstration to be
upheld primarily or only because of their pedagogical
effectiveness. It is rather that we can learn from the
Posterior Analytics how to present achieved knowledge and understanding to others only because of
what it primarily is: an account of what achieved and
perfected knowledge is.

Why do I say this? Not only because everything in the text is consistent with this view, but also
because Aristotle's system of thought requires just

such an account and it is nowhere else supplied. The *Physics* and the biological treatises report scientific enquiries which are still in progress, moving towards, but not yet having reached the *telos* appropriate to, and providing implicit or explicit guidance for, those specific types of activity. Clearly there must, on an Aristotelian view, be such a *telos*. And we need to know what it is, something only to be found, if anywhere, in the *Posterior Analytics*. So my claim is that the *Posterior Analytics* is an account of what it is or would be to possess, to have already achieved, a perfected science, a perfected type of understanding, in which every movement of a mind within the structures of that type of understanding gives expression to the adequacy of that mind to its objects.

Of course, in furnishing an account of what perfected and achieved understanding and knowledge are, Aristotle could not avoid the task of specifying, in part at least, the relationship between prior states of imperfect and partial understanding and that final state. And it was perhaps by attending too exclusively to what he tells us about this relationship and these prior states that earlier commentators were led to misconstrue Aristotle's intentions. But what matters about his discussions of understanding still in the process of formation, still in progress, in the *Posterior Analytics* is the light cast thereby on the way in which the *telos* of perfected understanding is already presupposed in partial understanding, and this is a concern very different from that of the *Physics* or of the biological treatises. So that when Aquinas in the introduction to his commentary distinguished the subject-matter of the *Posterior Analytics* from any concern with the nature of investigation, he correctly directed our attention to the place of the *Posterior Analytics* within Aristotle's works.

The *telos/finis* of any type of systematic activity is, on an Aristotelian and Thomistic view, that end internal to activity of that specific kind, for the sake of which and in the direction of which activity of that kind is carried forward. Many types of activity, of course, are intelligible as human activities only because and insofar as they are embedded in some other type of activity, and some types of such activity may be embedded in any one of a number of other types of intelligible activity. So it is, for example, with tree-felling, which may as an activity be part of and embedded in an architectural project of building a house or a manufacturing project of making fine papers or an ecological project of strengthening a forest as a habitat for certain species. It is these more inclusive and relatively self-sufficient forms of systematic activity which serve distinctive human goods, so that the *telos/finis* of each is to be characterized in terms of some such good. So the *Posterior Analytics* in its account of scientific demonstrative explanations as the *telos/finis* of enquiry furnishes us with an account of what it is to understand, that is, of the distinctive human good to be achieved by enquiry as a distinctive type of activity.

Achieved understanding is the *theoretical* goal of the *practical* activity of enquiry. Neither Aristotle nor Aquinas themselves discuss the theory of the practical activity of theoretically aimed enquiry in a systematic way, although some of Aristotle's discussions in the *Topics* are highly relevant and Aquinas rightly understood the *Topics* as a partial guide to such activity. Moreover, elsewhere in both Aristotle and Aquinas incidental remarks and discussions abound (see especially *Exposition of Boethius De Trinitate* VI, 1). But to make use of those remarks and discussion we must first say what, on the view taken by Aristotle and Aquinas, achieved understanding is. In so doing we shall find both that Aquinas, while generally endorsing Aristotle, goes beyond Aristotle's theses, and that later discussions of enquiry by nonAristotelian and nonThomistic writers can be put to good use in extending the Aristotelian account still further. So that although I shall be going over largely familiar and even over-familiar ground, it may not always be in an entirely familiar way.

A perfected science is one which enables us to understand the phenomena of which it treats as necessarily being what they are, will be and have been, because of the variety of agencies which have brought it about that form of specific kinds has informed the relevant matter in such a way as to achieve some specific end state. All understanding is thus in terms of the essential properties of specific kinds. What those kinds are, how they are to be characterized, what the end state is to which those individuals which exemplify them move or are moved, those are matters about which -- it seems plain from Aristotle's own scientific treatises as well as from modern scientific enquiry -- there may well have been changes of view and even radical changes of view in the course of enquiry. The final definition of these matters in a perfected science may be the outcome of a number of reformulations and reclassifications which have come about in the course of enquiry.

The mind which has achieved this perfected understanding in some particular area represents what it understands -- the form of understanding and the form of what is understood necessarily coincide in perfected understanding; that is what it is to understand -- by a deductive scheme in whose hierarchical structure the different levels of causal explanation are embodied. To give an explanation is to provide a demonstrative argument which captures part of this structure. What causal explanation enables us to distinguish is genuine causality from mere coincidence. The regularities of coincidence are striking features of the universe which we inhabit, but they are not part of the subject-matter of science, for there is no necessity in their being as they are. It follows from this account that in each distinctive form of achieved understanding, each science, there are a set of first principles, *archai/principia*, which provide premises for demonstrative arguments and which specify the ultimate causal agencies, material, formal, efficient and final for that science. It follows also that, insofar as the perfected sciences are themselves hierarchically organized, the most fundamental of sciences will specify that in terms of which everything that can be understood is to be understood. And this, as Aquinas remarks in a number of places, we call God.

There is then an ineliminable theological dimension -- theological, that is, in the sense that makes Aristotle's metaphysics a *theologia* -- to enquiry conceived in an Aristotelian mode. For enquiry aspires to and is intelligible only in terms of its aspiration to finality, comprehensiveness and unity of explanation and understanding, not only in respect of the distinctive subject-matters of the separate subordinate sciences, but also in respect of those more pervasive and general features of contingent reality, which inform those wholes of which the subject-matter of the subordinate sciences supply the constituent parts -- nature and human history. And, as the most radical philosophers of postEnlightenment modernity from Nietzsche to Richard Rorty have recurrently insisted, in the course of polemics against their less thorough-going colleagues, the very idea of a unified, even if complex, ultimate and final true account of the order of things in nature and human history has hidden -- and perhaps not so hidden -- within it some view of the relationship of contingent beings to some ground beyond contingent being.

What the substantive first principles which provide the initial premises of any perfected science achieve then is a statement of those necessary truths which furnish the relevant set of demonstrative arguments with their first premises, but also exhibit how if something is of a certain kind, it essentially and necessarily has certain properties. The *de re* necessity of essential property possession is represented in and through the analytic form of the judgments which give expression to such principles.[5] It is their analyticity which makes it the case that such principles are evident *per se*, but their evidentness is intelligible only in the context of the relevant body of perfected theory within which they function as first principles, and only an understanding of that body of theory will enable someone to grasp their analytic structure.

That first principles expressed as judgments are analytic does not, of course, entail that they are or could be known to be true *a priori*. Their analyticity, the way in which subject-expressions include within their meaning predicates ascribing essential properties to the subject and certain predicates have a meaning such that they necessarily can only belong to that particular type of subject, is characteristically discovered as the outcome of some prolonged process of empirical enquiry. That type of enquiry is one in which, according to Aristotle, there is a transition from attempted specifications of essences by means of prescientific definitions, specifications which require acquaintance with particular instances of the relevant kind (*Posterior Analytics* II, 8, 93a21-9), even although a definition by itself will not entail the occurrence of such instances, to the achievement of genuinely scientific definitions in and through which essences are to be comprehended. To arrive at the relevant differentiating causes which are specific to certain types of phenomena thus to be explained, empirical questions have to be asked and answered (*Posterior Analytics* I, 31 and 34, II, 19). But what results from such questioning is not a set of merely *de facto* empirical generalizations, but, insofar as a science is perfected, the specification through analytic definitions of a classificatory scheme in terms of which causes are assigned, causes which explain, in some way that subsequent enquiry cannot improve upon, the ordering of the relevant set of phenomena. So the analyticity of the first principles is not Kantian analyticity, let alone positivist analyticity. The first principles of a particular science are warranted as such if and only

if, when conjoined with whatever judgments as to
what exists may be required for that particular science, they can provide premises for a theory which
transcends in explanatory and understanding-
affording power any rival theory which might be
advanced as an account of the same subject-matter.
And insofar as the judgments which give expression
either to the first principles or to the subordinate
statements deriving from them, which together constitute such a theory, conform to how the essential
features of things are, they are called true. About
truth itself Aristotle said very little, but Aquinas has
a more extended account.

Truth is a complex property. "A natural
thing, therefore, being constituted between two
intellects, is called true with respect to its adequacy
to both; with respect to its adequacy to the divine
intellect it is called true insofar as it fulfills that to
which it was ordered by the divine intellect," and
Aquinas cites Anselm and Augustine and quotes
Avicenna. "But a thing is called true in respect of its
adequacy to the human intellect insofar as concerning it a true estimate is generated. . . ," and Aquinas
quotes Aristotle (*Quaestiones Disputatae De Veritate*
I, 2). The complexity of Aquinas's view is a consequence of his having integrated into a single account
theses both from Aristotle and Islamic commentary
upon Aristotle and from Augustine and Anselm. But
the integration is what is most important. Different

kinds of predication of truth each received their due within a genuinely unified theory of truth, in which the analogical relationship of different kinds of predication becomes clear.

What emerges then from the discussion of the rational justification of particular judgments within a perfected science by Aristotle in the *Posterior Analytics*, followed closely by Aquinas in his *Commentary*, and from the discussion of truth by Aquinas, in which Aristotelian theses are synthesized with Augustinian, is that both truth and rational justification have their place within a single scheme of perfected understanding and that the relationship between them depends upon their respective places within this scheme. But, as I emphasized earlier, what this conception of a perfected science supplies is a characterization of the *telos/finis* internal to and directive of activities of enquiry. What then is the nature of progress in enquiry towards this type of *telos/finis* and how are truth and rational justification to be understood from the standpoint of those still at early or intermediate stages in such a progress?

IV

In the progress towards a perfected science first principles play two distinct roles. Those which are evident to all rational persons do indeed provide standards and direction from the outset, but only when and as conjoined with initial sketches of those first conceptions and principles towards an ultimately adequate formulation of which enquiry is directed. Examples of the former type of first principle, evident to us as to all rational persons, are, of course, the principle of noncontradiction and the first principle of practical rationality, that good is to be pursued and evil avoided, and these are relatively unproblematic. But how are we even to sketch in outline at the outset an adequately directive account of a first principle or set of first principles, about which not only are we as yet in ignorance, but the future discovery of which is the as yet still far from achieved aim of our enquiry?

It is clear that, if we are able to do so, this will be the kind of case noticed earlier in which we shall be somehow or other already relying upon what we are not as yet fully justified in asserting, in order to reach the point at which we are fully justified in asserting it. But how then *are* we to begin? We can begin, just as Aristotle did, only with a type of dialectical argument in which we set out for criticism, and then criticize in turn, each of the established and best reputed beliefs held amongst us as to the fundamental nature of whatever it is about which we are enquiring: for example, as to the nature of motion in physics, or as to the human good in politics and ethics. As rival views are one by one discarded, leaving as their legacy to enquiry either something in them which withstood criticism or that which turned out to be inescapably presupposed by such criticism, so an initial tolerably coherent and direction-affording conception of the relevant first principle or principles may be constructed. The criticism of rival opinions about the human good in a way which leads on to an account of *eudaimonia* as that good in Book I of the *Nicomachean Ethics* is a paradigmatic case.

Yet, as enquiry progresses, even in these initial stages we are compelled to recognize a gap between the strongest conclusions which such types of dialectical argument can provide and the type of judgment which can give expression to a first principle. Argument *to* first principles cannot be demonstrative, for demonstration is *from* first principles. But it also cannot be a matter of dialectic and nothing more, since the strongest conclusions of dialectic remain a matter only of belief, not of knowledge. What more is involved? The answer is an act of the understanding which begins from but goes beyond what dialectic and induction provide, in formulating a judgment as to what is necessarily the case in respect of whatever is informed by some essence, but does so under the constraints imposed by such dialectical and

inductive conclusions. Insight, not inference, is
involved here, but insight which can then be further
vindicated if and insofar as this type of judgment provides just the premises required for causal explanation of the known empirical facts which are the
subject-matter of that particular science.

Moreover, the relationship between the different sciences and their hierarchical ordering
becomes important at this point. Initially the shared
beliefs which provide premises for dialectical arguments cannot but be beliefs prior to any particular
science; such are the beliefs criticized and corrected
in Book I of the *Nicomachean Ethics*. But once we
have a set of ongoing established sciences, the shared
set of beliefs to which appeal can be made include in
addition the beliefs presupposed in common by the
findings and methods of those sciences.[6] And what
those sciences presuppose are those judgments and
elements of judgments, understanding of which provides the key to Aristotle's metaphysical enterprise,
by directing his and our attention beyond the kinds of
being treated by the subordinate sciences to being
qua being.

Aristotle has sometimes been thought to
have undergone a radical change of mind between
the earlier *Posterior Analytics* and the later
Metaphysics, not least because in the first he denies
that there can be a supreme science, while in the latter he not only affirms there there can be, but pro-

vides it. Yet this discrepancy is less striking than at first seems to be the case. For what Aristotle means by what he calls "the demonstrative sciences" in the *Posterior Analytics* (e.g., I, 10, 76a37, 76b11-12) are such that none of *them* could be a supreme science: each is concerned with a distinct genus and each is demonstrative and any supreme science would have to be neither. So what Aristotle denied in the *Posterior Analytics* is not what he affirmed in the *Metaphysics*, and Aquinas who construed the relevant passages of the *Posterior Analytics* not as a denial of the possibility of a supreme science, but as a specification of its character had understood this very well (*Commentary on the Posterior Analytics*, lib. 1, lect. 17).

More than this, we can in this light now understand more adequately how dialectic even within the developing subordinate sciences can, by drawing upon those same presuppositions informing all scientific activity, bring us to the point at which the transition can be made from merely dialectical to apodictic and necessary theses. For the goal of such uses of dialectic thus reinforced is not to establish that there are essences -- that is presupposed, not proved, by dialectic and its further investigation is a matter for metaphysics -- but to direct our attention to how the relevant classifications presupposing essences are to be constructed, by providing grounds for deciding between the claims of rival alternative formulations of apodictic and necessary theses. Such theses cannot, as we have already noticed, *follow from* any dialectic conclusion any more than any law in the natural sciences can follow from the interpretation of any experimental result (and interpreted experimental and observational results often have in modern natural science the status assigned by Aristotle to dialectical conclusions), but they can be vindicated against their immediate rivals by such conclusions, just as formulations of natural scientific laws can be vindicated against rival formulations by experiment or observation.

We have then within any mode of ongoing enquiry a series of stages in the progress towards the *telos* of a perfected science. There will be dialectical conclusions both initially in the first characterizations of the *archê/principium* of that particular science, which provide the earliest formulations of the *telos/finis* of its enquiries, and later on in the arguments which relate empirical phenomena to apodictic theses. There will be provisional formulations of such theses, which in the light of further evidence and argument, are displaced by more adequate formulations. And as enquiry progresses the conception of the *telos* of that particular mode of enquiry, of the type of perfected science which it is its peculiar aim to achieve, will itself be revised and enriched.

Such a mode of enquiry will have two features which coexist in a certain tension. On the one hand, progress will often be tortuous, uneven, move enquiry in more than one direction and result in periods of regress and frustration. The outcome may even be large-scale defeat for some whole mode of enquiry. These are the aspects of enquiry not always recognized in adequate measure by either Aristotle or Aquinas and, consequently, their crucial importance to enquiry also needs a kind of recognition by modern Thomists which cannot be derived from our classical texts. Only types of enquiry, we have had to learn from C. S. Peirce and Karl Popper, which are organized so that they *can* be defeated by falsification of their key theses, can warrant judgments to which truth can be ascribed. The ways in which such falsification can occur and such defeat become manifest are very various. But in some way or other falsification and defeat must remain possibilities for any mode of enquiry and it is a virtue of any theory, and of the enquiry to which it contributes, that they should be vulnerable in this regard.

Hence, it was in one way a victory and not a defeat for the Aristotelian conception of enquiry when Aristotelian physics proved vulnerable to Galileo's dialectical arguments against it. And it is a mark of all established genuinely Aristotelian modes of enquiry that they too are open to defeat; that is, what had been taken to be adequate formulations of

a set of necessary, apodictic judgments, functioning
as first principles, may always turn out to be false, in
the light afforded by the failure by its own
Aristotelian standards of what had been hitherto
taken to be a warranted body of theory. And lesser
partial failures of this kind are landmarks in the history of every science.

So scientific progress is indeed not a
straightforward matter. But, on the other hand, it is a
central feature of enquiry, conceived as Aristotle and
Aquinas conceived it, that we should nonetheless
continue to think in terms of real and rational
progress within sciences towards the *telos/finis* of
each particular mode of enquiry. For it is in key part
in terms of their relationship to its specific *telos/finis*
that the theoretical statements which give expression
to what has been achieved in some particular enquiry
so far have to be characterized. Their status is a matter of how far and in what way they bring us closer to
that deductively organized body of statements which
would constitute the articulation in judgments of perfected understanding. But to understand better how
this is so, we must first look at the way in which, on
an Aristotelian and Thomistic view, enterprises
which issue in theoretical achievement are themselves practical enterprises, partially embedded in,
and having many of the central characteristics of,
other practical enterprises. Or to put the same point
in another way, the *Nicomachean Ethics* and the

Politics -- and correspondingly Aquinas's comment-
aries upon and uses of those works -- provide a context in terms of which the activities which resulted in
the various types of science described in the *Posterior
Analytics*, the *Physics* and the biological treatises --
and indeed in the *Metaphysics* and the *Summa
Theologiae* -- have to be understood.

So when Aristotle distinguishes genuine
enquiry, *philosophia*, from dialectic and sophistic
(*Metaphysics* 1004b17-26), he does so by contrasting
the *power* of philosophy with that of dialectic, but by
contrasting philosophy with sophistic as the project
(*prohairesis*) of a different life, that is, as a moral
contrast. And Aquinas comments that the
philosopher orders both life and actions otherwise
than does the practitioner of sophistic (*Commentary
on the Metaphysics*, lib. 4, lect. 4). So the life of
enquiry has to be structured through virtues, both
moral and intellectual, as well as through skills. It is
more than the exercise of a *technê* or a set of *technai*.
But in spelling out how this is so, we have to go
beyond what we are explicitly told by either Aristotle
or Aquinas.

The central virtue of the active life is the virtue which Aristotle names '*phronêsis*' and Aquinas
'*prudentia*.' Three characteristics of that virtue are
important for the present discussion. First, it enables
its possessor to bring sets of particulars under
universal concepts in such a way as to characterize

those particulars in relevant relationship to the good at which the agent is aiming. So it is a virtue of right characterization as well as of right action. Secondly, such characterization, like right action, is not achieved by mere rule-following. The application of rules may indeed be and perhaps always is involved in right characterization as in right action, but knowing which rule to apply in which situation and being able to apply that rule relevantly are not themselves rule-governed activities. Knowing how, when, where and in what way to apply rules is one central aspect of *phronêsis/prudentia*. These two characteristics of this virtue are sufficient to show its epistemological importance for enquiry; the lack of this virtue in those who pursue, and who teach others to pursue, enquiry always is in danger of depriving enquiry of the possibility of moving towards its *telos/finis*.

So enquiry involves not only a teleological ordering of the activities of enquiry, but also a teleological ordering of those who engage in it and direct it, at least characteristically and for the most part. And it is here that a third characteristic of *phronêsis/prudentia* as an epistemological virtue becomes important; both Aristotle and Aquinas stress the way in which and the degree to which the possession of that virtue requires the possession of the other moral virtues in some systematic way. In doing so they anticipate something of what was to be said about the moral and social dimensions of the natural sciences in one way by C. S. Peirce and in another by Michael Polanyi.

It is then within a social, moral and intellectual context ordered teleologically towards the end of a perfected science, in which a finally adequate comprehension of first principles has been achieved, that the Aristotelian and Thomistic conceptions of truth and rational justification find their place, and it is in terms of such an ordering that the relationships between them have to be specified. Consider now how they stand to each other, if we draw upon Aquinas's extended account.

The intellect, as we have already noticed, in this account completes and perfects itself in achieving knowledge. Truth is the relationship of the intellect to an object or objects thus known, and in predicating truth of that relationship we presuppose an analogy to the relationship of such objects to that which they were to be, that which they would be if they perfectly exemplified their kind. Rational justification is of two kinds. Within the demonstrations of a perfected science, afforded by finally adequate formulations of first principles, justification proceeds by way of showing of any judgment either that it itself states such a first principle or that it is deducible from such a first principle, often enough from such a first principle conjoined with other premises. For such perfected demonstrations express in the form of a scheme of logically related judgments the thoughts of an intellect adequate to its objects. But when we are engaged in an enquiry which has not yet achieved this perfected end state, that is, in the activities of almost every, perhaps of every science with which we are in fact acquainted, rational justification is of another kind. For in such justification what we are arguing to is a conclusion that such and such a judgment does in fact have a place in what will be the final deductive structure. We are engaged in the dialectical construction of such a structure, and our arguments will be of a variety of kinds designed first to identify the conditions which a judgment which will in fact find a place in the final structure must satisfy, and then to decide whether or not this particular judgment does indeed satisfy those conditions.

That truth which is the adequacy of the intellect to its objects thus provides the *telos/finis* of the activities involved in this second type of rational justification. And the deductively ordered judgments which provide the first type of justification with its subject-matter are called true in virtue of their affording expression to the truth of the intellect in relation to its objects, since insofar as they afford such expression they present to us actually how things are and cannot but be. Each type of predication of truth and each type of activity of rational justification stand in a relationship to others specifiable only in terms of their place within the overall

teleological ordering of the intellect's activities of
enquiry.

Those activities, it should be noted, involve a
variety of types of intentionality. And were we to
attempt to specify those intentionalities adequately,
we should have to learn not only from what Aquinas
says about intentionality, but from Brentano, Husserl
and, above all, Edith Stein. But it is important to
recognize that a Thomistic account of types of
intentionality, while it will be as much at variance
with those who wish to eliminate intentionality from
its central place in the philosophy of mind as are the
phenomenologists, will be an integral part of, and
defensible only in terms of, a larger Thomistic
account of the mind's activities, relating types of
intentionality to types of ascription of truth and of
rational justification, in an overall scheme of
teleological ordering. And any rational justification
of the place assigned to *archai/principia* in that perfected understanding which provides the activities of
the mind with its *telos/finis* is likewise inseparable
from the rational justification of that scheme of
teleological ordering as a whole.

There are, however, two objections which
may be advanced against understanding enquiry in
this Aristotelian and Thomistic mode. First, it may
be said that on the account which I have given no one
could ever finally know whether the *telos/finis* of
some particular natural science had been achieved or

not. For it might well appear that all the conditions
for the achievement of a finally perfected science
concerning some particular subject-matter had
indeed been satisfied, and yet the fact that further
investigation may always lead to the revision or
rejection of what had previously been taken to be
adequate formulations of first principles suggests
that we could never be fully entitled to make this
assertion.

My response to this objection is not to deny
its central contention, but rather to agree with it and
deny that it is an objection. The history of science
shows both in the case of geometry, which was widely
supposed to be a perfected science until the eigh-
teenth century, and in that of physics, supposed to be
approaching that state by Lord Kelvin and others in
the late nineteenth century, that this is an area in
which error is never to be ruled out. And it is
important that any philosophical account of enquiry
should be confirmed rather than disconfirmed by the
relevant episodes in the history of science.

We ought, however, at this point to note one
remarkable feature of Aquinas's account of enquiry,
one which differentiates it from Aristotle's. Aquinas,
like Aristotle, asserted that enquiry moves towards a
knowledge of essences, but unlike Aristotle he denies
that we ever know essences except through their
effects. The proper object of human knowledge is not
the essence itself, but the *quidditas* of the existent

particular through which we come to understand, so far as we can, the essence of whatever it is (*De Spiritualibus Creaturis* II, ad 3 and ad 7). So our knowledge is of what is, as informed by essence, but this knowledge is what it is only because of the nature of the causal relationship of the existent particular and its quiddity to the intellect.[7] Aquinas's affirmation of realism derives from this type of causal account. And such realism is quite compatible with a variety of misconstruals in their causal inferences by enquirers.

A second objection may appear to have been strengthened by my answer to the first. For I there appealed to the verdict of the history of science, and yet the history of science makes it plain, as do the histories of philosophy, theology and the liberal arts, that the actual course of enquiry in a variety of times and places has proceeded in a variety of heterogeneous ways, many of them not conforming to, and some radically at odds with, this philosophical account of enquiry, which I have tried to derive from Aristotle and Aquinas. But what point can there be, it may be asked, to a philosophical account of enquiry so much at variance with so much of what actually occurs, especially in specifically contemporary forms of intellectual activity?

The answer is that it is in key part by its power or its lack of power to explain a wide range of different types of episode in the history of science, the history of philosophy and elsewhere, including episodes which are from an Aristotelian and Thomistic standpoint deviant, that an account such as the Aristotelian and Thomistic account is to be tested. For if the Aristotelian view, as extended and amended by Aquinas, is correct, then specific types of departure from enquiry so conceived and specific types of denial of its central theses can be expected to have certain equally specific types of consequence. Intellectual failures, resourcelessnesses and incoherences of various kinds will become intelligible, as well as successes. A particular way of writing the history of science, the history of philosophy and intellectual history in general will be the counterpart of a Thomistic conception of rational enquiry, and insofar as that history makes the course of actual enquiry more intelligible than do rival conceptions, the Thomistic conception will have been further vindicated.

The *locus classicus* for a statement of how that history is to be written is the first and second chapters of Book A of the *Metaphysics*, supplemented by Aquinas's commentary. What Aristotle provides is not a narrative, but a scheme for the writing of narratives of that movement which begins from experience and moves through the practices of the arts and sciences to that understanding of *archai* which provides the mind with its terminus. And in succeeding chapters Aristotle writes a series of narratives, some very brief, some more extended, of those among his predecessors who failed or were only in the most limited way successful in their search for *archai*. At the same time Aristotle is providing indirectly a narrative of his own movement through the positions of his predecessors to his achievement of the positions taken in the *Metaphysics*. In doing so he reveals something crucial both about particular enquiries and about philosophical accounts of enquiry.

Of every particular enquiry there is a narrative to be written, and being able to understand that enquiry is inseparable from, implicitly or explicitly, being able to identify and follow that narrative. Correspondingly every philosophical account of enquiry presupposes some account of how the narratives of particular enquiries should be written. And indeed every narrative of some particular enquiry, insofar as it makes the progress of that enquiry intelligible, by exhibiting the course of its victories and its defeats, its frustrations and endurances, its changes of strategy and tactics, presupposes some ordering of causes of the kind that is only provided by an adequate philosophical account of enquiry.

Aquinas in his commentary endorses and amplifies Aristotle. Indeed, where Aristotle had said, referring to the early myths as precursors of science, that the lover of stories is in some way a philosopher, Aquinas says that the philosopher is in some way a

lover of stories. And at the very least, if what I have
suggested is correct, a philosopher will, in virtue of
his or her particular account of enquiry, always be
committed to telling the story of enquiry in one way
rather than another, providing by the form of narrative which he or she endorses a standard for those
narratives in and through which those engaged in
particular sciences cannot but try to make intelligible
both to themselves and to others what they are doing,
in what direction they are moving, how far they have
already moved and so on. Thomism, then, like all
other specific philosophical accounts of enquiry, has
implicit within it its own conception of how narratives of enquiry are to be constructed. Yet to intro-
duce the Thomistic conception of enquiry into contemporary debates about how intellectual history is
to be written would, of course, be to put in question
some of the underlying assumptions of those debates.
For it has generally been taken for granted that those
who are committed to understanding scientific and
other enquiry in terms of truth-seeking, of modes of
rational justification and of a realistic understanding
of scientific theorizing must deny that enquiry is constituted as a moral and social project, while those
who insist upon the latter view of enquiry have
tended to regard realistic and rationalist accounts of
science as ideological illusions. But from an
Aristotelian standpoint it is only in the context of a
particular socially organized and morally informed

way of conducting enquiry that the central concepts crucial to a view of enquiry as truth-seeking, engaged in rational justification and realistic in its self-understanding, can intelligibly be put to work.

To have understood this, and why the Thomist is committed to this way of understanding enquiry, is to have reached the point at which Thomism becomes able to enter certain contemporary philosophical debates by explaining, in a way that the protagonists of opposing standpoints within those debates are themselves unable to, how and why the problems posed within those debates are systematically insoluble and the rival positions advanced within them untenable. I do not, of course, mean that those protagonists would be willing or able to accept a Thomistic diagnosis of their predicament. Indeed, given the fundamental assumptions which have conjointly produced their predicament, it is safe to predict that to the vast majority of such protagonists it will seem preferable to remain in almost any predicament than to accept a Thomistic diagnosis. Nonetheless, it is only by its ability to offer just such a diagnosis, and one, as I have suggested, that will involve a prescription for writing intellectual history, that Thomism can reveal its ability to participate in contemporary philosophical conversation. What, then, is it that Thomism has to say on these matters?

V

Consider in a more general way than previously the unresolved disagreements and unsettled conflicts which characterize those contemporary philosophical theses, arguments and attitudes from which issue both the analytic and deconstructive rejection of first principles. Those disagreements and conflicts are, I want to suggest, symptoms of a set of underlying dilemmas concerning concepts whose status has, however, now been put in question in new and more radical ways.

So, for example, truth has been presented by some as no more than an idealization of warranted assertibility and by others as an entirely dispensable concept. Standards of warrant and justification have, as I noticed earlier, been relativized to social contexts, but the philosophers who have so relativized them have themselves been at odds with each other in multifarious ways. The intentionality of the mind's relationship to its objects, whether as understood by Thomists or otherwise, has been dismissed by some as a misleading fiction, while others have treated it as a pragmatically useful concept, but no more.

Debate over these and kindred issues has proceeded on two levels and on both it has been systematically inconclusive, perhaps in spite of, but perhaps because of the shared background beliefs of the protagonists of rival standpoints. At a first level, where debate has been directly about truth, rationality and intentionality, the difficulties advanced against earlier metaphysical conceptions -- conceptions dominant from the seventeenth to the nineteenth centuries -- have appeared sufficient to render such conceptions suspect and questionable for many different reasons, yet insufficient to render them manifestly untenable in any version, an insufficiency evident in the need to return again and again and again to the task of disposing of them. And so, at a second level, debate has opened up among those committed to rejecting or displacing or replacing such conceptions as to why what they have had to say has proved less conclusive in the arenas of philosophical debate than their protagonists had expected.

At this level too, disagreements are unresolved and rival views remain in contention. It has been argued, for example, that the antimetaphysical case has seemed less cogent than it is, because its protagonists have been insufficiently ruthless in purging their own positions of metaphysical residues. And it has been further asserted that, so long as the polemic against metaphysical conceptions of truth, rationality and intentionality is carried on in a conventional philosophical manner, it is bound to be thus burdened with what it ostensibly rejects, since the modes of conventional philosophy are inextricably tied to such conceptions. So the modes of conventional philosophical discourse must be abandoned. This is why Richard Rorty has tried to find a way of going beyond Davidson and Sellars.[8] This is in part why Derrida has had to go beyond Nietzsche and Heidegger.

Yet to follow Rorty and Derrida into entirely new kinds of writing would be to abandon the debate from which the abandonment of debate would derive its point. So there is a constant return to the debate by those who still aspire to discover an idiom, at once apt for negative philosophical purposes in refuting metaphysical opponents, but itself finally disentangled from all and any metaphysical implications. As yet they have failed.

This is a philosophical scene, then, of unsolved problems and unresolved disagreements, and perhaps it is so because these particular problems are in fact insoluble and these particular disagreements in fact unresolvable. Why might this be so? It is perhaps because within contemporary philosophy the concepts which generate these divisions occupy a distinctively anomalous position. They are radically discrepant with the modes of thought characteristic of modernity both within philosophy and outside it, so that it is not surprising that relative to those modes of thought they appear functionless or misleading or both. Yet they keep reappearing and resuming their older functions, most notably perhaps in those narratives of objective achievement in enquiry, by recounting which phil-

osophers make what they take to be the progress of
their enquiries, and the activities of debate which are
so central to that progress, intelligible to themselves
and to others.

Within such narratives at least, narratives of
a type which, so I suggested earlier, are essential con-
stituents of philosophical, as of all other enquiry, but
which nowadays are characteristically deleted and
even denied when the outcomes of such enquiry are
presented in the genre of the conference paper or the
journal article, there occurs a return of the
philosophically repressed, which reinstates for a
moment at least ways of understanding truth,
rationality and intentionality which it was a principal
aim of the philosophical activities recounted in the
narrative to eliminate. We may note in passing that it
is perhaps only in terms of their relationship to such
narratives -- narratives which still embody, even if in
very different forms the narrative scheme of Book A
of the *Metaphysics* -- that most contemporary philosophers are liable to lapse into something like a
teleological understanding of their own activities,
even if only for short times and on relatively infre-
quent occasions.

What I have asserted then is that there is a
tension between that in contemporary philosophy
which renders substantive, metaphysical or quasi-
metaphysical conceptions of truth, rationality and
intentionality not merely questionable, but such as to

require total elimination, and that in contemporary philosophy which, even when it is only at the margins of philosophical activity and in largely unacknowledged ways, prevents such total elimination. This thesis is capable of being sustained only insofar as it can be developed as a thesis about contemporary philosophy, elaborated from some standpoint external to the standpoints which dominate and define contemporary philosophy, for only thus can it be itself exempt from the condition which it describes. But from what point of view then can such a thesis be advanced? And, if it is from a point of view genuinely external to that of the kinds of philosophy which it purports to describe, how, if at all, can it be advanced as part of a conversation with the practitioners of those kinds of philosophy?

Ex hypothesi anyone who advances such a thesis must, it would seem, share too little in the way of agreed premises, beliefs about what is problematic and what is unproblematic, and indeed philosophical idiom with those about whose philosophical stances he or she is speaking. The depth of disagreement between the two parties will be such that they will be unable to agree in characterizing what it is about which they disagree. We are debarred, that is to say, from following Aristotle and Aquinas in employing any of those dialectical strategies which rely upon some appeal to what all the contending parties in a dispute have not yet put in question. How then are we to proceed? It is at this point that we have to resort to unThomistic means, or at least to what have hitherto been unThomistic means, in order to achieve Thomistic ends. What means are these?

Although I have identified the thesis which I have propounded about the nature of distinctively contemporary philosophy as one that can only be asserted from some vantage point external to that philosophy, I have up to this point left it, as it were, hanging in the air. I now hope to give it status and substance by suggesting -- and in this lecture I shall be able to do no more than suggest -- how, by being elaborated from and integrated into an Aristotelian and Thomistic point of view, it might become part of a theory about the predicaments of contemporary philosophy, providing an account of how those predicaments were generated and under what conditions, if any, they can be avoided or left behind.

The provision of such a theory requires the construction of something akin to what Nietzsche called a genealogy. The genealogical narrative has the function of not arguing with, but of disclosing something about the beliefs, presuppositions and activities of some class of persons. Characteristically it explains how they have come to be in some *impasse* and why they cannot recognize or diagnose adequately out of their own conceptual and argumentative resources the nature of their predicament. It provides a subversive history. Nietzsche, of course, used genealogy in an assault upon theological beliefs which Thomists share with other Christians and upon philosophical positions which Aristotelians share with other philosophers, so that to adopt the methods of genealogical narrative is certainly to adopt what have hitherto been unThomistic means. How then may these be put to the service of Thomistic ends?

What I am going to suggest is that the predicaments of contemporary philosophy, whether analytic or deconstructive, are best understood as arising as a long-term consequence of the rejection of Aristotelian and Thomistic teleology at the threshold of the modern world. I noticed earlier that a teleological understanding of enquiry in the mode of Aristotle and Aquinas has as its counterpart a certain type of narrative, one through the construction of which individuals are able to recount to themselves and to others either how they have achieved perfected understanding, or how they have progressed towards such an understanding which they have not yet achieved. But when teleology was rejected, and Aristotelian conceptions of first principles along with it, human beings engaged in enquiry did not stop telling stories of this kind. They could no longer understand their own activities in Aristotelian terms at the level of theory, but for a very long time they proved unable, for whatever reason, to discard that form of narrative which is the counterpart to the theory for narrative provided in the early chapters of *Metaphysics* A. It is thus unsurprising that, so long as this type of narrative survives in a culture, so long also Aristotelian and Thomistic conceptions are apt to recur even among those who believe themselves long since liberated from them.

So that one strand in the history of what followed upon the rejection of Aristotelian and Thomistic teleology would be an account of how, under the cover afforded by a certain kind of narrative, some Aristotelian and Thomistic conceptions survived with a kind of underground cultural life. Another and more obvious strand in that same history concerns the way in which in the history of philosophy and the history of science those conceptions were first displaced and marginalized, undergoing radical transformations as a result of this displacement and marginalization, and then even in their new guises were finally rejected. What were the stages in that history?

In the account which I gave of the Aristotelian and Thomistic account of enquiry, framed as it is in terms of first principles, I emphasized the way in which a variety of types of predication of truth and a variety of modes of rational justification all find their place within a single, if complex, teleological framework designed to elucidate the movement of the mind towards its *telos/finis* in perfected understanding, a movement which thereby presupposes a certain which they had discarded. It is only within the last hundred years that it has been recognized by those who have finally attempted to purge themselves completely of the last survivals of an Aristotelian conception of enquiry and of its goals that, in order to achieve this, narratives which purport to supply accounts of the movement of some mind or minds towards the achievement of perfected understanding must be treated as acts of retrospective falsification. But even those, such as Sartre, who have embraced this conclusion have themselves been apt to yield to the temptation to construct just such narratives, a sign of the extraordinary difficulties involved in repudiating this type of narrative understanding of the activities of enquiry.

It is not, of course, that such narratives themselves find an explicit place for distinctively Aristotelian, let alone Thomistic conceptions of truth, rationality and intentionality. It is rather that they presuppose standards of truth and rationality independent of the enquirer, founded on something other than social agreement, but rather imposing requirements upon what it is rational to agree to, and directing the enquirer towards the achievement of a good in the light of which the enquirer's progress is to be judged. These presuppositions can be elucidated in a number of different and competing ways, but it is difficult and perhaps impossible to do so without returning to just that type of framework kind of intentionality. It is within that framework and in terms of it that, not only are the functions of each kind of ascription of truth and each mode of rational justification elucidated, but also the relations between them specified so that what is primary is distinguished from what is secondary or tertiary and the analogical relationships between these made clear. Abstract these conceptions of truth and reality from that teleological framework, and you will thereby deprive them of the only context by reference to which they can be made fully intelligible and rationally defensible.

Yet the widespread rejection of Aristotelian teleology and of a whole family of cognate notions in the sixteenth and seventeenth centuries resulted in just such a deprivation. In consequence, conceptions of truth and rationality became, as it were, free floating. Complex conceptions separated out into their elements. New philosophical and scientific frameworks were introduced into which the older conceptions could be fitted only when appropriately and often radically amended and modified. And naturally enough conceptions which had been at home in Aristotelian and Thomistic teleological contexts in relatively unproblematic ways were now apt to become problematic and questionable.

Truth as a result became in time genuinely predicable only of statements; 'true' predicated of things came to seem a mere manner of speech, of no

philosophical interest. New theories of truth had,
therefore, to be invented, and they inescapably fell
into two classes: *either* statements were true in virtue
of correspondence between either them or the sen-
tences which expressed them, on the one hand, and
facts -- 'fact' in this sense is a seventeenth century
linguistic innovation -- on the other, *or* statements
were true in virtue of their coherence with other
statements. The protagonists of a multiplicity of rival
versions of correspondence and coherence theories
succeeded in advancing genuinely damaging critiques
of their rivals' theories and so prepared the way for a
further stage, one in which truth is treated either as a
redundant notion or as an idealization of warranted
assertibility.

In a parallel way conceptions of rational justification also underwent a series of transformations.
With the rejection of a teleological understanding of
enquiry, deductive arguments no longer had a place
defined by their function, either in demonstrative
explanations or in the dialectical constructions of
such explanations. Instead they first found a place
within a variety of epistemological enterprises, either
Cartesian or empiricist, which relied upon a pur-
ported identification of just the type of
epistemological first principle which I decribed earlier. When such enterprises foundered, a variety of
different and mutually incompatible conceptions of
rational justification were elaborated to supply what

this kind of foundationalism had failed to provide. The outcome was a *de facto* acknowledgment of the existence of a variety of rival and contending conceptions of rationality, each unable to defeat its rivals, if only because the basic disagreement between the contending parties concerned which standards it is by appeal to which defeat and victory can be justly claimed. In these contests characteristically and generally no reasons can be given for allegiance to any one standpoint rather than to its rivals which does not already presuppose that standpoint. Hence, it has often been concluded that it is the socially established agreement of some particular group to act in accordance with the standards of some one particular contending conception of rational justification which underlies all such appeals to standards, and that such agreement cannot itself be further justified. Where rationalists and empiricists appealed to epistemological first principles, their contemporary heirs identify socially established forms of life or paradigms or epistemes. What began as a rejection of the Aristotelian teleological framework for enquiry has, in the case of conceptions of truth, progressed through epistemology to eliminative semantics and, in the case of conceptions of rational justification, through epistemology to the sociology of knowledge.

What I am suggesting then is this: that certain strands in the history of subsequent philosophy are best to be understood as consequences of the rejection of any Aristotelian and Thomistic conception of enquiry. To construct the genealogy of contemporary philosophy -- or at least of a good deal of contemporary philosophy -- in this way would disclose three aspects of such philosophy which are otherwise concealed from view. First, such a genealogical account would enable us to understand how the distinctive problematic of contemporary philosophy was constituted and what its relationship is to the problematics of earlier stages in the history of modern philosophy. The history of philosophy is still too often written as if it were exclusively a matter of theses and arguments. But we ought by now to have learned from R. G. Collingwood that we do not know how to state, let alone to evaluate such theses and arguments, until we know what questions they were designed to answer.

Secondly, once we understand how the questions and issues of contemporary philosophy were generated, we shall also be able to recognize that what are presented from within contemporary philosophy as theses and arguments about *truth as such* and *rationality as such* are in fact theses and arguments about what from an Aristotelian and Thomistic standpoint are degenerated versions of those concepts, open to and rightly subject to the radical critiques which have emerged from debates about them, only because they were first abstracted from the only type of context within which they are either fully intelligible or adequately defensible. Hence, in important respects Thomists need have no problem with much of the contemporary critiques; if indeed truth and rationality were what they have for a long time now commonly been taken to be, those critiques would be well-directed. And in understanding this the Thomist has resources for understanding contemporary philosophy which the dominant standpoints within contemporary philosophy cannot themselves provide.

To this, however, it may well be retorted that the protagonists of those standpoints have no good reason to concede that the history of modern philosophy should be construed as I have attempted to construe it, even if they were to grant for argument's sake that the very bare outline sketch which I have provided could in fact be filled in with the appropriate details. Nothing in their own beliefs, it may be said, nothing in the culture which they inhabit gives them the slightest reason to entertain any conception of enquiry as teleologically ordered towards an adequate understanding of an explanation in terms of *archai/principia*. They, therefore, cannot but understand the sixteenth and seventeenth century rejections of Aristotelianism, whether Thomistic or otherwise, as part of a progress towards greater enlightenment. And in this perspective the accounts which they have given of truth, rationality and intentionality are to be understood as culminating achievements in a history of such progress. Where the Thomist sees stages in a movement away from adequate conceptions of truth and rationality, stages in a decline, the protagonists of the dominant standpoints in contemporary philosophy, so it will be said, will see stages in an ascent, a movement towards -- but the problem is: towards what?

The defender of contemporary philosophy is at this point in something of a dilemma. For if he or she can supply an answer to this last question -- and it is not too difficult to think of a number of answers -- what he or she will have provided will have been something much too like the kind of narrative account of objective achievement in enquiry whose structure presupposes just that type of teleological ordering of enquiry the rejection of which is central to the whole modern philosophical enterprise. But if he or she cannot supply an answer to this question, then philosophy can no longer be understood to have an intelligible history of achievement, except in respect of the working out of the details of different points of view. It will have become what David Lewis has said that it is: "Once the menu of well-worked out theories is before us, philosophy is a matter of opinion . . . ."[9] Yet, the question arises once again about *this* conclusion: is it an achievement to have arrived at it or not? Is it superior in truth or rational warrant to other opinions? To answer either 'Yes' or 'No' to these questions revives the earlier difficulty.

It is no part of my contention that a protagonist of one of the dominant trends in contemporary philosophy will lack the resources to frame a response to this point, adequate in its own terms. It is my contention that such a protagonist will even so lack the resources to explain the peculiar predicaments of contemporary philosophy and to provide an intelligible account of how and why, given its starting-point and its direction of development, to be trapped within these predicaments was inescapable. Thomism enables us to write a type of history of modern and contemporary philosophy which such philosophy cannot provide for itself.

In the course of writing this kind of genealogical history Thomism will be able to open up possibilities of philosophical conversation and debate with standpoints with which it shares remarkably little by way of agreed premises or shared standards of rational justification. It will be able to do so insofar as it can show how an Aristotelian and Thomistic conception of enquiry, in terms of first principles and final ends, can provide us with an understanding and explanation of types of philosophy which themselves reject root and branch the possibility of providing a rational justification for any such conception. But that is, of course, work yet to be done. In this lecture

I have not even come near to showing that in fact it can be done. All that I have been able to do is to sketch in bare outline some suggestions for a way of initiating this enterprise in the hope that it may be less barren than attempts to initiate philosphical conversation between Thomists and protagonists of standpoints in contemporary philosophy have proved to be in the past.

Endnotes

1. See Mark Jordan, *Ordering Wisdom* (Notre Dame, 1986), pp. 118-119. I am deeply indebted to Mark Jordan and Ralph McInerny for their assistance at various points.

2. See, e.g., *Of Grammatology*, translated by G. C. Spivak (Baltimore, 1976), p. 65 and the discussion by Peter Dews in chapter 1 of *Logic of Disintegration* (London, 1987).

3. See, e.g., chapter 3 of *Reason, Truth and History* (Cambridge, 1981).

4. See "Aristotle's Theory of Demonstration" in *Articles on Aristotle*, edited by J. Barnes, M. Schofield and R. Sorabji, Volume I (London, 1975).

5. For an overview of disputed questions on this topic and a view at some points different from mine, see chapter 12 of R. Sorabji, *Necessity, Cause and Blame* (London, 1980).

6. The book which states the central issues most fully is T. H. Irwin, *Aristotle's First Principles* (Oxford, 1988); I suspect that, if my account were less compressed, it would be more obviously at variance with Irwin's.

7. See chapter 8 of E. Gilson, *Thomist Realism and the Critique of Knowledge*, translated by M. A. Wauck (San Francisco, 1986), especially pp. 202-204.

8. See R. Rorty, *Contingency, Irony and Solidarity* (Cambridge, 1989), pp. 8-9.

9. See *Philosophical Papers*, Volume I (Oxford, 1983), pp. x-xi.

The Aquinas Lectures
Published by the Marquette University Press
Milwaukee, Wisconsin 53233
United States of America
= =

#1 **St. Thomas and the Life of Learning.** John F. McCormick, S.J. (1937).

ISBN 0-87462-101-1

#2 **St. Thomas and the Gentiles.** Mortimer J. Adler (1938).
ISBN 0-87462-102-X

#3 **St. Thomas and the Greeks.** Anton C. Pegis (1939).
ISBN 0-87462-103-8

#4 **The Nature and Functions of Authority.** Yves Simon (1940).
ISBN 0-87462-104-6

#5 **St. Thomas and Analogy.** Gerald B. Phelan (1941).
ISBN 0-87462-105-4

#6 **St. Thomas and the Problem of Evil.** Jacques Maritain (1942).

ISBN 0-87462-106-2

#7 **Humanism and Theology.** Werner Jaeger (1943).
ISBN 0-87462-107-0

#8 **The Nature and Origins of Scientism.** John Wellmuth (1944).
ISBN 0-87462-108-9

#9	**Cicero in the Courtroom of St. Thomas Aquinas.** E. K. Rand (1945).
	ISBN 0-87462-109-7

#10	**St. Thomas and Epistemology.** Louis Marie Regis, O.P. (1946).
	ISBN 0-87462-110-0

#11	**St. Thomas and the Greek Moralists.** Vernon J. Bourke (1947).
	ISBN 0-87462-111-9

#12	**History of Philosophy and Philosophical Education.** Etienne Gilson (1947).
	ISBN 0-87462-112-7

#13	**The Natural Desire for God.** William R. O'Connor (1948).
	ISBN 0-87462-113-5

#14	**St. Thomas and the World State.** Robert M. Hutchins (1949).
	ISBN O-87462-114-3

#15	**Method in Metaphysics.** Robert J. Henle, S.J. (1950).
	ISBN 0-87462-115-1

#16	**Wisdom and Love in St. Thomas Aquinas.** Etienne Gilson (1951).
	ISBN 0-87462-116-X

#17	**The Good in Existential Metaphysics.** Elizabeth G. Salmon (1952).
	ISBN 0-87462-117-8

#18   **St. Thomas and the Object of Geometry.** Vincent Edward Smith (1953).

ISBN 0-87462-118-6

#19   **Realism and Nominalism Revisited.** Henry Veatch (1954).
ISBN 0-87462-119-4

#20   **Imprudence in St. Thomas Aquinas.** Charles J. O'Neil (1955).
ISBN 0-87462-120-8

#21   **The Truth that Frees.** Gerard Smith, S.J. (1956).
ISBN 0-87462-121-6

#22   **St. Thomas and the Future of Metaphysics.** Joseph Owens (1957).

ISBN 0-87462-122-4

#23   **Thomas and the Physics of 1958 A Confrontation.** Henry Margenau (1958).

ISBN 0-87462-123-2

#24   **Metaphysics and Ideology.** William O. Martin (1959).
ISBN 0-8746S-124-0

#25   **Language, Truth, and Poetry.** Victor M. Hamm (1960).
ISBN 0-87462-125-9

#26   **Metaphysics and Historicity.** Emil L. Fackenheim (1961).
ISBN 0-87462-126-7

#27   **The Lure of Wisdom.** James D. Collins (1962).
ISBN 0-87462-127-5

#28   **Religion and Art.** Paul Weiss (1963).
ISBN 0-87462-128-3

Uniform format, cover, and binding.

Copies of this Aquinas Lecture and the others in the series are obtainable from:

Marquette University Press
Marquette University
Milwaukee, Wisconsin 53233, U.S.A.

Publishers of:

*Medieval Philosophical Texts in Translation
*Pere Marquette Theology Lectures
*St. Thomas Aquinas Lectures
*Philosophy & Theology (journal)

DATE DUE